stress at work: causes, effects and prevention

a guide for small and medium sized enterprises

EF/94/13/EN

Members of the scientific committee of the conference "Stress at work – A call for action", Brussels, 9/10 November 1993:

Dr. Jaume Costa,
European Foundation, Dublin;

Ms. Dagmar Diergarten,
Confederation of German Employers' Associations, Cologne;

Dr. Ronald Haigh,
Commission of the European Communities, Luxembourg;

Prof. Marc Heselmans,
Ministry of Labour, Brussels;

Prof. Robert A. Karasek,
University of Massachusetts, Lowell;

Dr. Michiel Kompier,
TNO Prevention and Health;

Prof. Lennart Levi,
Karolinska Institute, Stockholm;

Mr. Henrik Litske,
European Foundation, Dublin;

Mr Eduardo Mardaras Platas,
Mutua General, Barcelona;

Dr. Vittorio Di Martino,
International Labour Office, Geneva;

Dr. Salvador Moncada,
Occupational Health Centre of Barcelona;

Mr. Pascal Paoli,
European Foundation, Dublin;

Mr. Marcel Wilders,
Netherlands Trade Union Confederation, Amsterdam.

stress at work: causes, effects and prevention

a guide for small and medium sized enterprises

by

Michiel Kompier and

Lennart Levi

European Foundation
for the Improvement of Living and Working Conditions

Loughlinstown House, Shankill, Co. Dublin, Ireland

Tel: +353 1 282 6888 Fax: +353 1 282 6456

Telex: 30726 EURF EI

Cataloguing data can be found at the end of this publication

Luxembourg: Office for Official Publications of the European Communities, 1994

ISBN 92-826-8594-2

Printed in Ireland

PREFACE

Stress has become a major issue, but the word "stress" is used by different people, in different contexts and for different purposes. This makes it sometimes difficult to understand precisely to what stress actually refers. The first aim of the present booklet is to clarify what stress is and the consequences it might have.

Its second aim is to go one step further by providing companies, employees, their representatives, and all other interested parties with some short and practical guidelines to identifying stressful factors and starting action to eliminate sources of stress at the workplace.

The Foundation asked the authors to take into account existing handbooks, and other guidelines and practices which have been developed in the member states of the European Union and others, so as to offer a "European" approach to stress prevention.

We would like to thank the authors for their enthusiasm in their endeavours and efforts to produce a practical, user-friendly and down-to-earth booklet. We would also like to thank the members of the Scientific Committee of the European conference "Stress at work – a call for action" who have provided feedback which helped us in preparing the booklet.

Clive Purkiss, *Director*	Eric Verborgh, *Deputy Director*

CONTENTS

CHAPTER 1

INTRODUCTION

Stress at work – does it concern *you*? And, if so, how, and why? Is there anything you can do to identify its causes and consequences?

And, with regard to these causes and consequences – should you see them as 'God-made', as a stroke of fate, and impossible to influence? Does it follow that noxious conditions of work should be accepted, tolerated and adapted to? Or should such conditions be improved, wherever possible, and their consequences – in terms of occupational stress and disease – ameliorated, or even prevented? And, last but not least, shouldn't conditions which promote health and well-being at work be promoted?

This booklet aims to answer these and related questions in a manner understandable to the lay reader but, at the same time, based on solid scientific evidence. Its other important aim is to enable you, the reader, not only to identify sources of your own stress at work, and its causes and consequences in terms of health and well-being, but also to cope actively with at least some of these causes and consequences.

This booklet has been prepared to suit a wide variety of working conditions in twelve different countries. It follows that you, the reader, must choose from our small 'menu' that which applies to your individual conditions, expectations, abilities and needs.

Using a metaphor – should you, doing this, simply adjust your 'feet' to the 'shoes' provided by the employer, i.e. to your conditions of work? Or should you instead aim at doing it conversely, namely adapting these 'shoes' to your 'feet'?

Chapter 2

What is Stress?

2.1 *Stress*

John, 36, married and a father of two children, works in a small factory, at an assembly line. In traditional occupational environment terms, it is a good place to work at. The noise created by the machinery has been reduced to an acceptable level. Illumination is good. Temperature, flow, and humidity of the air have been adjusted to norms. John is seated in a comfortable chair, and his working posture has been adjusted to avoid unnecessary loads and twists. The risk for occupational accidents is low to negligible.

In spite of all this, John feels sad, anxious, and, indeed, ill. He smokes, drinks, and eats too much. He has difficulties falling asleep in the evening, and wakes up early, feeling tired and frustrated. His wife worries about his recurrent headaches, chronic indigestion, and increase in blood pressure, as diagnosed by their family doctor. She is appalled every time he states that 'life is not worth living anymore'.

How has all this come about? Let's take a closer – and broader – look.

Facing considerable difficulties on the labour market, John's employer has laid off some 30% of his staff, streamlining the production process ('lean production'), and urging all his workers to 'work harder', and if necessary, longer hours, overtime. The work itself has remained highly monotonous, with a small number of simple tasks being repeated again, and again, and again. The recent lay-offs have caused uneasiness among the workers with mutual suspicion, hostility, and reluctance to help one another. Everyone is afraid of being next in line for being laid off. In this highly competitive setting, and with performance paid by individual piece wages, fewer and fewer are prepared to lend a helping hand to their fellow workers. This sums up a situation characterized by high demands in *quantitative* terms (too much to do) and low demands in *qualitative* terms (too simple and unstimulating work), combined with low *decision latitude* (possibilities to decide what is to be done, and how), and *low social support* from fellow workers. This combination spells *stress*, and, consequently, an increased risk of physical and mental occupational ill health, causing suffering, absenteeism, decreased productivity, and losses to employees and employers alike.

This is not an extreme case. It is part of every-day life for a considerable proportion of workers and salaried employees in countless small and medium-sized enterprises in Europe, and elsewhere.

Our key questions are: (1) why is this so; and (2) can we – and you, the reader – do something to improve the situation?

In engineering, stress is 'a force which deforms bodies'. In medicine, the term refers to your body's strategy for adapting to whatever influences, changes, demands, and strains it encounters. This strategy swings into action if you are assaulted on the street or insulted by your boss, expected to achieve something you feel unable to do, or when, with or without cause, you worry about your job. Stress is caused by a multitude of demands and exposures (stressors), such as an inadequate fit between what you need and what you are capable of getting, and what your environment offers to you and what it demands of you, at work and elsewhere. You need a certain amount of responsibility, but your job offers less or demands more. You do need a certain amount of work, but you often get too much, or you are threatened with unemployment, and actually get none at all.

Another cause of stress lies in role conflicts. We all play several roles. We are husbands or wives; we are parents to our children, we are children to our parents; we are brothers or sisters, friends; and we are bosses, peers and subordinates – all at the same time. And the ingredients of conflict are easy to find in trying to fill these multiple roles.

There is something common to all these cases in the way the body attempts to adapt. This common denominator – a kind of 'revving up' or 'stepping on the gas' – is stress. Some level of stress is always to be found in the body, just as, to draw a rough parallel, a country maintains a certain state of military preparedness even in peacetime. Occasionally this preparedness is intensified, sometimes with good cause, at other times without.

In this way, the stress level affects the rate at which processes of wear and tear in the body take place. The more 'gas' given, the higher the RPMs at which the body's engine is driven, the more rapidly the 'engine' wears out. Or, to take another metaphor, if you burn a candle with a high flame, or at both ends, it will burn down more quickly. However, the problem is not that the body reacts to stress; what matters is the degree of stress, i.e., the rate of wear and tear, how often, and for how long the body is under stress.

Sometimes it is difficult to determine whether stress in a particular situation is good or bad. Take, for instance, the exhausted athlete on the winner's stand, or the newly appointed but stress-racked executive. Both have achieved their goals. In terms of pure accomplishment, one would have to say that the result was well worth the effort. In psychological terms, however, this is more doubtful, since a good deal of torment may have been needed to get so far – long years of training, or incessant overtime, at the expense of family life. From the medical viewpoint, they perhaps burnt their candles at both ends. The athlete may rupture a muscle or two, the executive may develop high blood pressure, or a heart attack.

2.2 *Is stress harmful?*

The answer is: yes and no. It all depends on the situation in which it occurs. For example, a car stops at a traffic light and its driver 'steps on the gas'. In response, the engine races, leading to increased wear and deposition of soot on the valves, without the car moving from the spot. On the other hand, stepping on the gas while driving on a motorway may be sensible and productive. Stress in this medical sense (adapting) cannot be eliminated. Without it, the process of life would cease, for the absence of stress means death. What needs to be avoided is stress in the engineering (deforming) sense. The relevant questions are: 'How great is it, and is it appropriate to the needs of the situation?'

Your sense of control over what is happening to you is also critical. When you feel in control, stress becomes the spice of life, a challenge instead of a threat. When you lack this crucial sense of control, stress can spell crisis – bad news for you, your health and your enterprise.

Suppose that you have been called upon to reverse a falling trend in the sales of a major product and have been given a short time to do so. To make things worse, your enterprise or even the entire market is beset by serious problems. Weeks go by, and despite your increasingly desperate efforts, sales are still down and the forecast is bleak. Like Sisyphus, you keep pushing the rock up the hill, only to see it slide down again. This is stress in capital letters.

Breaking down the causes of occupational stress one step further, we arrive at the following list, based more on experience than on theoretical considerations (cf. Rosch, 1984).

– Inadequate time to complete the job to one's satisfaction.

– Lack of clear job description or chain of command.

– Absence of recognition or reward for good job performance.

– Inability or lack of opportunity to voice complaints.

– Lots of responsibilities but little authority or decision-making capacity.

– Uncooperative superiors, co-workers, or subordinates because of basic differences in goals and values.

– Lack of control or pride over the finished product.

– Job insecurity due to pressures from within or possibility of takeover or merger.

– Exposure to prejudice and bigotry due to age, gender, race, ethnicity, or religion.

– Unpleasant environmental conditions because of smoking, crowding, noise and air pollution, exposure to toxic chemicals or carcinogens, or commuting difficulties.

– Concerns related to one's responsibility for other employees.

– Not being able to utilize personal talents or abilities effectively or to full potential.

– Chances for a small error or momentary lapse of attention to have serious or even disastrous consequences.

2.3 *Stress reactions*

When we are exposed to these or related stressors – which often boil down to a lack of control over our work combined with excessive demands, unsatisfied needs, unfulfilled expectations, overstimulation, understimulation, role conflicts and lack of social support and recognition – most of us experience 'dysphoric' reaction such as anxiety, depression, uneasiness, apathy and alienation. These reactions may not be entirely avoidable, but the intensity and frequency of their occurrence are critical.

Stress can also cause us to behave in unhealthy or otherwise inappropriate ways. Some of us start (or increase) smoking or overeating. We may seek comfort in alcohol or take unnecessary risks at work or in traffic. Aggressive, violent or other types of antisocial behaviour may be the outlet chosen. Many of these reactions can lead to disease and premature death. Suicide is one of many examples.

We may also react physiologically. Take, for example, the employee who feels unjustly criticized by his or her supervisor. The employee's typical reactions are increased blood pressure, increased or irregular heart rate, muscular tension, with subsequent pain in the neck, head, and shoulder, dryness of throat and mouth, and overproduction of acid gastric juice.

2.4 *Stone-age*

These psychological and physiological reactions are of very ancient origin if we consider the evolution of mankind. When assessing the human organisms reactions, we tend to forget that man lived in the forest for millions of years, has worked in the fields for thousands and in the factories for hundreds of years, at the most, and has been sitting in front of computer terminals for no longer than about 30 years. When confronted with actual physical danger – e.g. a wolf pack – the stone-age savage reacted with both fear and physical activation – for fight or flight. This was a highly appropriate response in the stone age 'work environment' and helped the individual and the species to survive, in the face of immediate dangers.

Since then, man's working environment and the demands made on him have changed radically. But his 'physical make-up' and reactions are largely unaltered. We seldom need to react in this stone-age way nowadays, as we rarely meet physical threats. But we still retain our tendency to react with an increase in blood pressure, excessively rapid heartbeat, fast or deep respiration, muscular tension, and by mobilizing various 'fuels', even to the anticipation or *threat* of danger which may never materialise and the *memory* of dangerous events that occurred long ago.

2.5 *Health effects*

Disturbances in bodily functions commonly found in people exposed to stressful situations at work include:

– muscular symptoms such as tension and pain;

– symptoms from the stomach and intestines, such as indigestion, vomiting, heartburn, constipation and irritation of the large intestine;

– symptoms from the heart and the blood vessels, such as palpitation, arrhythmias and chest pain;

– lung symptoms such as difficulty in breathing or abnormally fast or deep respiration;

-central nervous system symptoms such as functional disorders of the mind or emotions, disturbed sleep, weakness, faintness and headaches;

– sexual problems, such as painful menstruations, frigidity and impotence.

Not only do these symptoms cause the worker much distress and suffering, they also entail high cost to the community and very considerable losses in work time and productivity for the employer.

2.6 *Control as a critical factor*

How much 'say' an employee has in his/her job is a critical factor. In a study on 1600 Swedish men, heart disease symptoms were most common (with 20% of the workers affected) among those who described their work as both psychologically demanding and with a low degree of decision-making latitude. By contrast, workers who reported low psychological demands and a high level of skill discretion had no symptoms of heart disease. Their jobs were associated with a much better state of health than that of the average worker.

A number of studies in different countries have shown a relationship between exposure to occupational stressors (such as high psychological demands at work combined with low decision-making latitude and low level of social support) and presumably work-related illness and death rate. This evidence is strong enough to justify measures to prevent or reduce stress.

Chapter 3

Who is Vulnerable?

People are different. Every person has his or her own individual characteristics and peculiarities, and weak and strong sides. Differences arise through 'nature' and 'nurture'.

Some determinants of individual susceptibility to stress are 'Type A' personality, coping ability, and social support. Other determinants are age, gender, and present illness or state of chronic disability.

3.1. *'Type A' personality, coping ability and social support*

People with a so called 'Type A personality' tend to lead a highly competitive, hectic way of life, combining hostility, speed, impatience and obsessive concern with doing more and more in less and less time, and with no opportunity or ability for unwinding and recuperation. In organizations, Type A's often are respected for their motivation, dedication and accomplishments, but they may be disliked for their impatience, unfriendliness and lack of cooperation. Organizations may support these employees by setting clear goals (to prevent them from developing higher standards than they are able to meet), and by stimulating cooperation above competitiveness (by rewarding their cooperation more than their individual performance).

The 'Type A' example illustrates that much depends not only on what we are exposed to, but also on how we *cope* with the situation. Coping refers to totally different ways of behaviour. We can change our environment, eliminate the cause of a problem, flee from it, ask for help, accept things as they are or bury our head in the sand and deny the problem. Generally, coping refers to two different strategies, on the one hand altering the *situation* and on the other hand altering the *perception* of the situation (without changing it). The particular ways of coping influence the stress reaction. However, there is no 'ideal' coping behaviour. The effectiveness of coping behaviour depends on the circumstances, the situation, and the targets. Coping behaviour that reduces stress in the short term (for example smoking a cigarette) may be harmful in the long term. Coping behaviour that is stressful in the short term (for example asking your boss for a better work plan) may be valuable in the long term.

However consistently people seem to cope, they are able to learn, to change their coping behaviour, to behave differently in different situations. Differences between employees could make organizations dynamic, flexible and even innovative.

Another important factor influencing our vulnerability is our access to, and utilization of, social support – from our partner, child, friends or workmates. Such support may bolster our self-esteem, help us to appraise realistically what we are exposed to, offer us crucially important feelings of belonging, and offer practical and tangible support.

3.2. *Young workers and elderly workers*

With *young workers* the key problem today is the high youth unemployment rate throughout Europe. It has been shown that this may lead to increases in tobacco and alcohol consumption (particularly in young males), to psychosomatic symptoms like headache and stomachache (particularly in young females), and dysphoric reactions (anxiety, depression, restlessness) and antisocial attitudes.

However, young people who succeed in finding a job have their problems as well. On entering the labour market they often have no choice and may be forced to accept a job that is not compatible with their abilities and ambitions. Often these jobs offer high risks for stress at work: high mental and physical demands and low control.

Elderly workers could be at risk for several reasons. Some older workers simply have to work in jobs where the risk of exploitation is great, where exposure to harmful conditions of work is high and where protection is low or absent, or they will not get any job at all. Secondly, higher age usually enhances general vulnerability and may be accompanied by physical impairments, for example in heart and lung functioning, in musculo-skeletal injuries or in limited hearing or vision. Usually these impairments have minor or no consequences at all for the ability to work, unless in jobs which are physically highly demanding. It is necessary that the elderly get adequate opportunities, for example changes in tasks and responsibilities and access to courses and training in new skills. A good policy to keep the elderly healthy and in good shape is to start with the young!

This is a fitting place to remind you, the reader, of another important problem area, namely, the right to work at all. But how can this right be ensured, in a time when computers and robots are taking over more and more of working life, when the economy is stagnating, when cutbacks are ravaging the public sector, and international competition from low wage countries is growing steadily fiercer? One answer is surely by planning work 'with people in mind', and by maintaining a sense of solidarity at both the group and personal levels. Another possibility is that those who have jobs can share them in one way or another with those who do not: we could, for example, consent to pay higher taxes, accept lower wages and profits, or shorter working hours. The burden, of course, must be commensurate with the capacity of each and all – both workers and employers – to bear it. A third possibility is to empower and train the unemployed to enable them to find, or create, new jobs, individually or cooperatively, and to facilitate such initiatives.

3.3 *Migrant workers*

A third category comprises *migrant workers* who face the challenge of adapting to a wide variety of new conditions, including differences in climate, eating habits, social customs, cost of living, housing facilities, and type and rhythm of work. They may be disabled in dealing with these changes by their inexperience of urban life and by their inadequate knowledge of the language of the country. Their cultural background, customs and traditions often create a barrier to their integration in the host country. Such factors have an important influence on migrant worker behaviour and can predispose to ill health. The prevalence of psychiatric disorders seems to be two to three times as high among recent migrants as among the local population. Psychosocially induced stress may manifest itself in various physical disorders, particularly of the stomach and intestines.

In studies in some countries, it was found that the accident rate is 2.5 times as high in migrant workers as in nationals. The occupational accident rate was found to be 92 per 1,000 foreign workers, compared with 32 per 1,000 native workers.

Many companies have implemented successful programmes to facilitate a better integration of migrant workers. These programmes include language and vocational training, special provisions for food and religious holidays, prevention and control of racial discrimination and xenophobia at the workplace, among others. A multicultural workforce shows the public and customers the commitment of the company towards equal opportunity policy.

3.4. *The disabled*

A fourth group at risk – *the disabled* – is much more complex and difficult to define. This is due to the fact that a handicap should always be considered in relation to the work at which the individual is expected to function. As the environmental setting varies enormously not only from community to community, but also from one enterprise to another, the importance of any single handicap or pattern of handicaps will differ according to the environmental opportunities and demands and compensatory potentials in the individual. Suffice it to say that millions of Europeans are severely physically, mentally or socially disabled. Examples of such groups are those with impaired vision or hearing, the disabled, the mentally retarded or ill, and drug addicts and alcoholics.

Again, increased vulnerability often coincides with increased exposure to the most vicious environments. Noise, pollution, overcrowding, nutritional deficiencies and low hygienic standards characterise some huge industrial areas as well as settlement areas in the slums of many developed countries. To these very areas, various segregational forces 'select' exactly those individuals who are most in need of a more favourable environment. In this way, maximal vulnerability is combined with maximal exposure to environmental stressors, increasing the risk of a subsequent decline in health and well-being below the subsistence level.

Often the disabled suffer from their physical or mental handicap, but suffer even more from the prejudices of their employers or colleagues. Fortunately, there are many examples of good practice, employers without prejudices who hire disabled people for their good qualities. While taking into account their disabilities, they concentrate on knowledge, abilities, skills and motivation. Sometimes subsidies are available to provide for necessary adaptations in the working environment.

3.5. *Female workers*

Most countries have had, and many still have, labour regulations which forbid the employment of women in certain jobs. Reasons given include the lower physical strength of women; the desire by women or men to protect home and family life; and the desire to protect pregnant women, particularly during the early stages of pregnancy. The second of these factors is conditioned by social norms and reflects society's concept of 'what is right for a woman to do'. The other two, however, are based on physiological evidence. One additional obstacle that easily creates stress in women is the fact that many women, in addition to working full time, also have to carry the burden of the full responsibility for housework and/or rearing of the children. In extreme cases this means that women may have to work more or less without interruption for say, 14 hours a day, seven days a week. The only obvious factor that undoubtedly leads to increased vulnerability in the female relates to pregnancy. Pregnant women, or rather their unborn children, run special risks when they are exposed to, for instance, ionising radiations, toxic chemicals, vibrations and arduous physical effort. Apart from these cases, however, there is nothing to prove that women are more sensitive than men to harmful substances and the onslaughts of the environment.

So it is remarkable that many European women joining an organization have to face all kinds of problems which basically have nothing to do with their physical characteristics. They often encounter prejudice, get less attractive jobs, get lower wages for the same jobs, and have fewer opportunities for developing a career. At the workplace they will find themselves mainly in the lowest positions with the least power. In a corporate culture which is dominated by men they are liable to discrimination and sexual harassment. Besides, women may have a different appraisal of the workplace. While men may appreciate power, competitiveness and personal achievement, women may value a congenial atmosphere, cooperation and team work.

Consequently both men and women could contribute to a balanced working organization. For successful cooperation between men and women, an equal opportunity policy is required in all aspects of company life, i.e. remuneration, career development, promotion, training etc. Sexual harassment should be banned. Arrangements for child care can help women to cope with 'double jobs', as can the provision of flexible working times and parental leave facilities for men and women.

Chapter 4

The Reasons for Stress Monitoring by Small and Medium-Sized Enterprises (SMEs)?

4.1 *Five reasons for paying attention to stress at work*

1. Stress is a problem for the worker and the company.

As is shown in previous chapters, stress can lead to psychological disorders (such as exhaustion, depression), diseases of the heart and the blood vessels, stomach and intestinal diseases, and musculoskeletal diseases (mainly back problems). The result could well be illness, sickness, absenteeism and even work disability.

For employers, absenteeism through illness causes considerable problems as regards planning, logistics and personnel. Stress, therefore, results in a loss of production and can lead to a poor work climate.

2. Work stress problems are on the increase.

In many countries, the scale of problems related to work stress is on the increase. One reason is that the character of work has changed dramatically in the past decades. All kinds of tasks which traditionally required muscle power now call for mental effort instead. Computerization of the production process has made a large contribution to this development. Also, the intensity of work has increased. In many countries, the work rate has been steadily increased and a smaller number of employees must achieve the same, or even higher, output. Reorganizations, technological changes and flexibility of production and services are the order of the day, in both the private and public sectors. For many employees this gives rise to insecurity. Knowledge is also becoming ever more quickly outdated.

3. It is a legal obligation.

The EU Framework Directive on Health and Safety compels the employer to recognise stress factors and to correct them. This Framework states, amongst other things, that the employer has 'a duty to ensure the safety and health of workers in every aspect related to the work, following general principles of prevention: avoiding risks, evaluating the risks which cannot be avoided, combating the risks at source, adapting the work to the individual, especially as regards the design of work places, the choice of work equipment and the choice of working and production methods, with a view, in particular, to alleviating monotonous work and work at a predetermined work-rate and to reducing their effect on health'.

In addition to this legislation at EU level, numerous EU member states have legislation concerning the physical and psychosocial work environment.

One example is the Working Environment Act in the Netherlands. This Working Environment Act is aimed at improving the level of safety in the workplace and improving the mental and physical health and the well-being of employees. It applies to all employed persons, both in the private and public sector, whether in large, medium-sized or small companies. As to the psychological aspects of the working situation – the well-being part of the legislation – it is stated that:

– 'Employees should be able to organize their own work in accordance with their own professional qualifications'

– 'Employees should have sufficient opportunity to determine their own work pace'

– 'Each employee has the right to be informed about the purpose and the results of his or her work'

– 'Employees should have sufficient opportunity to keep in contact with their colleagues'

– 'The workplace should be laid out in accordance with modern ergonomic principles'

– 'Monotonous and repetitive jobs should be avoided'

– 'Differences between the workers' personal characteristics, such as age, gender, physical and mental constitution, work experience, skills and knowledge of the working language, should be taken into account'

– 'Safety and health hazards must, as far as is practicable, be prevented at the source'.

It is stated in this law that the employer is responsible for the work environment. Employees also have a certain responsibility for their own safety and health, and they are obliged to cooperate on health and safety matters with their managers.

Another example is the amended Swedish Work Environment Act (1991).

This act now states the following concerning the characteristics of the work environment:

– 'Working conditions shall be adapted to people's differing physical and psychological circumstances'

– 'The employee shall be enabled to participate in the arrangement of his or her own job situation as well as in work on changes and developments that affect his or her own job'

– 'Technology, work organization and job content shall be arranged so that the employee is not exposed to physical or mental loads that may cause ill health or accidents'

– 'The matters to be considered in this context shall include forms of remuneration and the scheduling of working hours'

– 'Rigorously controlled or tied work shall be avoided or restricted'

– 'It shall be the aim for work to afford opportunities for variety, social contacts and cooperation as well as continuity between individual tasks'

– 'It shall be the aim for working conditions to afford opportunities for personal and occupational development as well as for self-determination and occupational responsibility.'

4. Harmful stress can be avoided, since it is to a large extent work-related.

Research has clearly shown that stress is, to a large extent, determined by the working situation. However, in addition, causes can also originate from outside the working situation, such as 'stressful life events'. These are far-reaching personal events such as the death of your partner, divorce, personal injury or disease. Of course, as was shown in the previous chapter, personality traits can also play a role: being too demanding of yourself, setting your ambitions too high, displaying overly aggressive and competitive behaviour and not reserving sufficient time for relaxation ('Type A'). It is hardly possible for employers to exert influence on such life events or behaviour patterns. What they can do is to 'root out stress risks in the work situation' or limit these as far as possible. That is in the interests of both the employees and the enterprise. Effective stress management results in a more productive work organization, reduced absenteeism, an improved quality of work, and better occupational health and well-being.

5. Nowadays organisations are facing major changes.

There is increased competition in the European market without frontiers and with the countries outside the Community: United States of America, Japan and South-East Asia. Needs for improved productivity and quality, innovations in technology and work organisation, environmental requirements, and changes in the workforce (ageing, multi-cultural, women) demand flexibility and adaptability. Therefore a workforce is required which is willing to change and innovate, which is customer-oriented and highly motivated. Stress prevention at work would be highly conducive to such a development.

Chapter 5

What are the Instruments for Monitoring Stress at Company Levels?

5.1 *A monitoring strategy*

Since the implementation of the Framework Directive for Health and Safety in national legislation, all companies must monitor health and safety risks at the workplace. As stress is a major health and safety risk, it would be wise to include stress indicators in the monitoring system.

As stress is closely related to control, it is important to involve employees in the monitoring from the very beginning. If workers are not well informed, not involved in the how and why, and do not know what will happen with the results, the monitoring itself could be a major stressor causing distrust and resistance.

Recognition of employees' expertise on their own work situation and the work organisation in general will be beneficial for the workers as well as the organisation.

Monitoring means systematically searching for risk factors (stressors, as mentioned in chapter 2) and risk groups. Risk groups are employees in jobs with high demands, low control, low support and/or health problems. Also, as was described in chapter 3, young workers and elderly workers, migrant workers, the disabled, and female workers might (but need not necessarily) be vulnerable groups.

In monitoring, the main emphasis is on work factors and not on individual differences among workers. This does not mean that individual differences among people do not play an important role in the development of stress. There are, after all, considerable differences among people. What could be a challenge to you could well be a source of stress for another employee. You could further ask yourself why, in the same situation, one employee suffers stress while the other does not. Often, employers have a tendency to emphasise these differences. If employees have health complaints or are absent because of illness, some employers are quick to say it is caused by personal problems within the home, for example. The causes are generally thought to lie in the individual employee. Little attention is paid to possible relationships among these domestic problems, health problems and the work itself. This kind of reasoning generally leads to the employee being regarded as 'guilty' of his own health problems: 'blaming the victim'. Logically, this has consequences for the recommendations which are made by some employers to reduce stress. They may accordingly concentrate more on the individual employee, and 'coping with stress', than on changing the stressful conditions.

In fact, the same reasoning can be applied here as in the case of safety risks. One construction site is more dangerous than another. And not every building trade worker runs the same risks. Building trade workers who refuse to wear a safety helmet, even though these are provided by the company, and do not stay alert in high-risk situations, run more risks than others. Some workers are more strongly committed to work safety than others. Primarily, however, it is still the task of the company to prevent unsafe situations. Employees should then also 'act safely'.

This book focuses upon the differences among working situations more than on the differences among individuals. If occupational group A shows a great deal of absenteeism because of stress, and occupational group B does not, then we raise the question whether that difference is caused by that occupation, and, if so, how we can track down the causes.

5.2 *The whole company, departments or positions?*

A company is made up of departments and positions. This is the case for medium-sized enterprises and frequently also for smaller organizations. You could take the whole company as a unit for analysis. However, this creates the danger that a possible problem department (or problem position) is not spotted. If you, for example, look at the figures for absenteeism due to illness for the whole company, then the high absenteeism of one problem department might be obscured by the low absenteeism rates of other departments.

Statistics about the whole company are particularly useful:

– to compare the whole company with its own departments;

– to compare the company with similar companies in the same branch.

In order to find which stress signals there are in your company, you will have to collect information at both the company and departmental level.

You may also be interested in the stress problem of only one particular department or position (e.g. a nursing ward or the nurses in a hospital). In this case as well, you can use the following instruments (checklists, questionnaires and analyses of administrative data) for that specific group of employees.

5.3 *Four checklists*

Of all instruments, checklists are the most practical for this purpose. Checklists are actually multiple-choice lists in which possible problems in the working situation, as described in previous chapters, can be reported. This book will discuss four checklists which can be used to investigate smaller companies, as well as departments and positions in larger companies (Kompier & Marcelissen 1990). The four checklists are:

- Checklist Job Content (e.g. monotonous work, emotionally demanding work, time pressure, lonely jobs, incorrect work organization, insufficient support and information)
- Checklist Working Conditions (e.g. high or disturbing noise levels, dangerous situations, bad ergonomic lay-out)
- Checklist Terms of Employment (insufficient career opportunities and training, unfair remuneration, bad planning of working and resting periods, problems with overtime, piece wages)
- Checklist Social Relations at Work (e.g. insufficient work consultation system, bad psychological atmosphere, discrimination, sexual harassment).

None of the above checklists can be regarded as a fully validated scientific instrument. They are, however, useful aids which have been designed according to modern scientific principles and are helpful in obtaining a clear picture of your own working situation and that of your fellow workers or employees. Your first step is to refer to your organization plan and determine which positions or departments you wish to investigate (or have investigated). The organization plan is a diagram which depicts the structure of the organization and indicates the various hierarchical levels (such as: management, middle management, staff departments and operational personnel).

There are various ways in which to proceed:

a) Using the checklists, you personally investigate the departments or positions concerned. You can also have that done by an 'occupational health specialist' (such as a company doctor or personnel manager) or by a project team, which could even be specially formed for that purpose.

b) You use the checklist as a guideline in interviews which you hold with representatives from the particular departments or positions.

c) You have the checklist filled in by representatives from the departments or positions concerned.

d) You allow the checklists to be filled in by the employees concerned, for example, during work consultations or a group meeting.

The checklists are included as Appendix 1 (see page 56). Low scores reflect a favourable situation. The higher the total scores, the larger the number of problems. In fact, every single tick calls for attention within the workplace.

5.4 *Questionnaires*

In medium-sized companies, questionnaires can also be used to trace occupational stress. A questionnaire can focus on the working situation ('causal factors or stress risks') and on stress-related health problems ('the consequences of stress').

Questionnaires are generally filled in by individual employees and then analyzed on a group level. For example, employees from various departments indicate whether they have any health complaints. Subsequently the average score for each department is calculated. These average scores become more reliable as more persons per department fill in the questionnaire. The groups should not be too small, otherwise random chance will have too great an influence, and real effects can't be reliably detected. Also, in this case, confidentiality could be violated. It should therefore be considered as a rule of thumb that the groups which are to be compared should include at least 15 respondents and that the respondents complete the questionnaires voluntarily and anonymously.

Questionnaires generally require professional support in their administration, the processing of the data and the interpretation of the results. For professional support you might approach occupational health psychologists from the nearest University or occupational health services.

The questionnaire in Appendix 2 (page 65) makes it possible to map out stressful factors in the working situation. This list includes parts of the Job Content Questionnaire by Robert Karasek (1985), and also questions from two other stress questionnaires. These are the Dutch Work and Health Questionnaire (Smulders et al. 1992), and NOVA-WEBA (Dhondt & Houtman 1992; Houtman et al. 1994). Some demographic questions are also included – such as gender, age, and education – in order to facilitate the search for possible risk groups (e.g. younger workers, older workers) and to compare men and women.

Appendix 3 (page 71) contains the Health Complaints Questionnaire, which is a translation of the Dutch Questionnaire VOEG (Dirken 1969). Consisting of thirteen questions, this questionnaire helps you to determine stress-related health complaints.

5.5 *Administrative data*

In medium-sized companies, an analysis of administrative data can also provide an insight into the possible consequences of stress. The most important data in this context are those concerning absenteeism through illness, turnover and work disabilit). In assessing these data, one should constantly be asking whether there is any relation between, for example, sickness absenteeism and the working situation. In fact, the question whether there are reasons to consider certain high absenteeism rates as being work-related is always important. For example, do departments with high absenteeism rates also produce unfavourable scores on the aforementioned checklists and questionnaires? Do departments in which a relatively high number of employees leave the company at their own request within a few years, score unfavourably on the Job Content and Social Relations at Work checklists?

Of course, there is no simple 'one-to-one relationship' between sickness absenteeism and work stress. There are many reasons, other than work-related, why people become ill. You should therefore always be careful not automatically to equate absenteeism through illness or work disability to health damage, or always expect to find its causes at work. However, all that being said, it has been proven in various studies that a considerable percentage of absenteeism through illness is in fact work-related.

When analyzing sickness absenteeism, one should not report on groups which are too small or periods which are too short. Basically, the group size should be 15 or more and the figures should refer to a whole year. Other useful administrative measures are:

- Productivity rates
- Number of accidents
- Data concerning overtime
- Backlogs in taking days off, etc.

By comparing a number of annual data, possible trends can be found over the years.

Chapter 6

Who Does the Monitoring?

6.1 *Organizational commitment*

The detection of work stress and implementation of measures to counter its causes and consequences can only be done successfully when there is wide-ranging support within the company for tackling stress. Stress monitoring is not merely a technical process. In most cases cooperation among the various 'company parties' is the key issue. That means that all 'parties' consider it worthwhile to work together on a stress project: (top) management, employees, trade unions, personnel department, company doctor and individual employees. If there is no real commitment from these parties, then there is a high risk that an initiated stress project will not be successful and fail in its final objectives (i.e. fewer complaints and absenteeism, an improved working environment, a better and more efficient work organization).

The promotion of healthy working conditions is, in the first place, the (legal) responsibility of the employer. Often this can be stimulated by trade unions, work councils, and health and safety committees. They, for example, may use the checklists that were described in the previous chapter to get stress placed on the company agenda.

6.2 *Who is to do the monitoring and which instruments are to be used?*

There is no one simple detector of stress. It is therefore wisest to use several of the methods mentioned above. In this manner, the evidence is collected from a variety of sources.

The methods mentioned above vary from relatively simple to somewhat more sophisticated. Which persons in small and medium-sized companies and institutions can now apply these instruments? That depends to some extent on the level of know-how which is available in the company in the areas of occupational safety, health and welfare.

When you are working in a small company there generally will not be an 'in-house' specialist on health and safety matters. Nor will such a company usually have a personnel department. But its lines of communication are mostly short and the required information can often be collected in a reasonably informal manner. One person, e.g. a manager, can be made responsible for collecting information, for example with the use of checklists.

A medium-sized company will often have a larger staff department, but may not, for example, have a company doctor. In many cases, the monitoring of stress signals can take place from within these staff departments, e.g. by the personnel manager.

The following can be said concerning the usefulness and applicability of the instruments under discussion:

– **Checklists:**

No specialised knowledge is needed for applying these. They are also highly suitable for use by the employees themselves in order to 'check' their own workplace.

– **Questionnaires:**

Small companies generally benefit very little from the use of questionnaires. A discussion, for example during the work consultation meetings where the checklists are used as a guideline, is more practical and informative.

In larger companies, the questionnaires can provide an insight into problems on the level of department, position or company; comparisons can then be made within the company and with other companies.

However, before having the questionnaires filled in, it is important that the following points are clearly stated:

- What are the objectives of filling in the questionnaires?
- How will the results be reported, and to whom?
- Who will be asked to fill in the lists?
- Is the report to be made public?
- Who will collect data, analyse them and process them into a report?
- Are the lists anonymous or named; if named, for what reason?
- Are there guarantees against premature and/or unauthorised disclosure, or infringements on employee privacy?
- How long will the data be stored?

– **Administrative data:**

This is only of use in the somewhat larger companies. Sometimes, these have access to automatic data files ('Personnel Information Systems').

Chapter 7

Prevention of Stress at Work

7.1 *Introduction*

In order to prevent stress there are three basic strategies in order of preference:

1. Eliminate or modify the stress-producing situation or remove the individual from it. Find 'the right shoe for the right foot', or allow the person concerned to adjust the 'shoe' to fit his or her 'foot'.

2. Adjust the 'shoe' – that is, change the work – to fit the individual's 'foot'.

3. Strengthen the person's resilience to stress, for example, through physical exercise, meditation and relaxation techniques, and social support.

The first two kind of strategies are directed at the working situation. The third strategy is person-oriented.

Stress management has traditionally focused on individual approaches, usually by counselling individuals or small groups of employees on ways to adapt to, or cope with, various occupational stressors and/or their consequences. More recently, approaches have started to encourage the employee to adjust his/her work environment to his or her abilities and needs, improving the person-environment fit, and advising management and supervisors to allow or even promote such adjustments.

7.2 *Measures directed at the working situation*

Some of the more important adjustments proposed for your consideration – and your employer's – are the following ten, based on formulations by Paul Rosch (1984):

1. Allow adequate time for satisfactory work performance.
2. Provide clear job description.
3. Reward good job performance.
4. Provide ways to voice complaints; consider them seriously and swiftly.
5. Harmonize responsibility and authority.
6. Clarify goals and values of the enterprise; adapt them to employees' goals and values whenever possible. Why do we work? For what common goals?
7. Promote employee control and pride over end product (goods, services).
8. Promote tolerance, security, and justice at work.

9. Eliminate harmful physical exposures.
10. Identify failures, successes, and their causes and consequences; learn how to avoid the failures and how to promote the successes – learn from experience.

Additional, partly overlapping, issues proposed by the US National Institute of Occupational Safety and Health (NIOSH) and based on Swedish, Dutch, and other experiences and recommendations, are:

– *Work schedule*. Design work schedules to avoid conflict with demands and responsibilities unrelated to the job. Schedules for rotating shifts should be stable and predictable, with rotation in a forward (morning-afternoon-night) direction.

– *Participation/control.* Allow workers to provide input for decisions or actions affecting their jobs.

– *Workload.* Ensure assignments are compatible with the capabilities and resources of the worker, and allow for recovery from especially demanding physical or mental tasks.

– *Content.* Design tasks to provide meaning, stimulation, a sense of completeness, and an opportunity to use skills.

– *Roles.* Define work roles and responsibilities clearly.

– *Social environment.* Provide opportunities for social interaction, including emotional support and help directly related to one's job.

– *Future.* Avoid ambiguity in matters of job security and career development.

Four general categories of approaches and strategies proposed by NIOSH can be applied in any community:

1. Improve job content and organization in order to control psychosocial risk factors at work.

2. Monitor changes in work situation, workers' health and their interrelationship.

3. Increase awareness, inform, train, educate.

4. Broaden goals and strategies of occupational health services.

But most importantly, we must create for ourselves and for others those occupational and other situations which give our lives meaning, content and structure, as well as identity, self-esteem, companions, friends and material means.

7.3 *Person-oriented measures*

By following the principles mentioned above we can adjust our 'shoe' to our 'foot'. However, this may take time or even turn out not to be feasible in the short run. Here, we need to resort to the complementary strategy of adjusting the 'foot' to the 'shoe', by physical exercise and/or relaxation techniques, medication and counselling.

Physical exercise is often beneficial because it helps us to burn up the pent-up energy produced in the stress reaction. Instead of hitting our boss or running away from our mate, we kick a football or take a jog in the woods. The pent-up tension finds a release. The increased heart work and higher blood lipid content is put to good use. Correspondingly, a number of *relaxation methods*, e.g. autogenic training, yoga, transcendental meditation, etc., may be used to help us to unwind and to reduce our body's propensity to react with stress.

Medication may in selected cases be needed. Some act on the brain, affecting mental and/or emotional functions, and thereby indirectly affecting the organ symptoms (e.g. excessively rapid heartbeat) which accompany these functions (e.g. in anxiety states); other drugs block the stream of nervous impulses from the brain to various organs (e.g. by decreasing heart reactivity to such nervous stimuli). Both these types of drugs may help some individuals considerably. They can diminish a person's reaction to various stressors. But of course they can never remove these stressors, or replace actual improvements in the organization of work or in the work environment. Use of medication must always be prescibed by a physician.

In *counselling*, your doctor or therapist endeavours, by means of conversations and other forms of mental influencing, to change those harmful attitudes and ways of responding which predispose a person to stressor-exposures or to inadequate reactions to unavoidable exposures.

Most of us are able to patch up a surface graze or a scratch ourselves. Similarly, everyone should be able to administer the simplest form of mental assistance, for which the term 'psychological first-aid' has been coined. Such first aid is easy to apply. The basic point is to give the person in need of help the chance to speak his mind; even just being able to do so is experienced as a great relief by most. Once they are formulated in words, problems are not so vague and terrifying, get structure and become easier to cope with. On the other hand, one should be a little sparing with 'good advice', for to give such advice, one must have a much more thorough knowledge of the fellow worker's situation than a layman generally possesses. The best help one can offer is quite simply to listen, calmly, patiently and with sympathy.

7.4 *Ten hints for your individual stress management*

1. Learn to recognize your stress reactions. See them as a warning. Perhaps to ease up? Have a day off? Consult a doctor? Try to change your job?

2. Try to pinpoint the immediate cause of stress – work, family, money? Are you demanding too much of yourself? Is there something you can/want to change? How can you bring about such a change?

3. Perhaps you tend to be stressed by trifles, things that are soon forgotten and not worth getting worked up about. Don't 'rev up' over small worries. Don't sweat over the small stuff! They are just worries, not disasters.

4. Don't torment yourself with the 'what ifs'. As someone remarked: 'My life has been full of worries. Most of them about things that never happened'.

5. When there is something which you cannot do anything about, don't run at it head on. Just hold your breath and let it come. If you can't fight or flee – flow with the situation until you can do something about it!

6. Look elsewhere for compensation – in your family, if the going is tough at work; or at work, if family life is shaky.

7. Give – and accept – social support. Share one another's burdens.

8. Find out what is real. Be realistic in your ambitions. And avoid fighting ghosts.

9. Exercise regularly to expend the pent-up energy produced by stress. Avoid hard liquor and cigarettes.

10. Try to gain control of your life. Change whatever should and can be changed. Accept what cannot be changed. And find compensation for the latter.

CHAPTER

8

CONCLUSIONS

Stress is a major threat to modern organisations. However, much can be done to prevent it. It is necessary that every organisation recognises the causes of stress, mainly organisational factors, although individual factors should not be excluded. Stress prevention should be primarily aimed at balancing job demands and control, while social support is an important way to relieve work-related stress, which cannot be avoided. Special attention for specific groups at risk might be necessary.

Successful prevention of stress requires a systematic approach and worker involvement in all stages, i.e. planning, monitoring, risk assessment, choosing a strategy, implementing improvements and evaluation.

But please, do not wait for another occasion, or for someone else to act. Act yourself. And start now!

BIBLIOGRAPHY

– **Cohen, A., Levi, L., Pardon, N. & Kalimo, R.**: *Psychosocial factors at work: Recognition and control,* International Labour Office, Geneva (1986)

– **Dhondt, S. & Houtman, I.L.D.**: *NOVA-WEBA (in Dutch),* TNO Institute for Preventive Health Care, Leiden (1992).

– **Dirken, J.M.**: *Dutch Questionnaire VOEG (in Dutch),* TNO Institute for Preventive Health Care/Wolters Noordhoff, Groningen (1969)

– **Dunckel, H. & Zapf, D.**: *Psychischer Stress am Arbeitsplatz. Belastungen, gesundheitliche Folgen, Gegenmassnahmen.* Bund-Verlag, Köln

– **European Foundation (Paoli, P.)**: *First European Survey on the Work Environment 1991-1992.* European Foundation for the Improvement of Living and Working Conditions, Dublin (1992)

– **Houtman, I.L.D., Bloemhoff, A., Dhondt, S. & Terwee, C.**: *WEBA and NOVA-WEBA related to health and well-being of employees* (in Dutch). The Hague (1994)

– **International Labour Office, Conditions of Work Digest**: *Preventing stress at work, Volume 11, 2,* Geneva (1992)

– **Kalimo, R., El-Batawi, M.A., Cooper, C.L. (Eds.)**: *Psychosocial factors at work and their relation to health,* World Health Organization, Geneva (1987)

– **Karasek, R.**: *Job Content Questionnaire and Users Guide* (1985)

– **Karasek, R. & Theorell, T.**: *Healthy work. Stress, productivity, and the reconstruction of working life,* Basic Books, New York (1990)

– **Keita, G.P. & Sauter, S.L. (Eds.)**: *Work and Well-being – An Agenda for the 1990s.* American Psychological Association, NIOSH, Washington (1992)

– **Kompier, M.A.J. & Marcelissen, F.H.G.**: *Handbook Work Stress* (in Dutch), Dutch Working Environment Institute-NIA, Amsterdam (1990)

– **Kompier, M.A.J., Marcelissen, F.H.G., Vaas, S.**: *Stress at the workplace? Do something about it!* (in Dutch). FNV/CNV/MHP, Amsterdam (1990)

– **Levi, L.**: *Psychosocial factors in preventive medicine.* In: Hamburg, **D.A., Nightingale, E.C. & Kalmar, V. (Eds.)**, *Healthy people: The Surgeon General's report on health promotion and disease prevention:* Background papers (p.207-252). U.S. Department of Health, Education and Welfare/Public Health Service, Washington D.C (1979)

– **Levi, L. (Ed.)**: *Society, Stress and Disease – Working Life.* Volume 4, Oxford University Press, Oxford (1981).

– **Levi, L.**: *Preventing work stress.* MA: Addison-Wesley, Reading (1981)

– **Levi, L., Frankenhaeuser, M. & Gardell, B**. *Work stress related to social structures and process*. In: **Elliott, G.R. & Eisdorfer (Eds.)**, *Stress and human health: Analysis and implications of research (pp.119-146)*, Springer, New York

– **Levi, L.**: *Stress in industry – Causes, Effects and Prevention.* International Labour Office, Geneva (1984).

– **Rosch, P.J.**: *The health effects of job stress.* Business and Health, May Issue, pp. 5-8 (1984).

– **Smulders, P.G.W., Winter, C.R. de & Gründemann, R.W.M.**: *The Dutch Work and Health Questionnaire,* TNO Institute for Preventive Health Care, Leiden (1992).

– **World Health Organization:** *A healthier work environment – basic concepts and methods of measurement.* WHO, Copenhagen (1993)

Appendices

Checklists and Questionnaires

Appendix 1

Appendix 2

Appendix 3

APPENDIX 1. *Four Checklists*

A. CHECKLIST JOB CONTENT

The Checklist Job Content contains 19 questions which can be answered by every department. With a little editorial adaptation, the questions can also be applied to every position.

Fill in 'yes' if you agree with the question. Subsequently, a total score can be calculated by adding up the 'yes' scores. The total score must be as low as possible. The higher the number of 'yes' answers, the greater the number of problems in the area of job content and the organization of work. Every 'yes' answer deserves separate attention.

		Yes	No
1	Short cyclical work is common. A task is short cyclical if the same task repeatedly has to be started within 1.5 minutes of the last task; that is when the cycle is shorter than one and a half minutes.	☐	☐
2	Dull or monotonous tasks are common (these are tasks which quickly become routine).	☐	☐
3	Tasks which require intense concentration (from which one cannot withdraw oneself) are common.	☐	☐
4	The work in the department is strongly segmented. Every individual makes a small contribution to the 'product' of the department.	☐	☐
5	The work is emotionally demanding, for example, because of contacts with patients, customers, pupils and the like.	☐	☐

		Yes	No
6	Work frequently takes place under the pressure of time, deadlines have to be met, or the production standards are difficult to achieve.	☐	☐
7	There are lonely jobs in the department.	☐	☐
8	It frequently occurs that the organization of the work and/or the work schedules are incorrect.	☐	☐
9	It frequently occurs that the other departments do not prepare the work sufficiently.	☐	☐
10	It frequently occurs that the other departments do not provide sufficient support.	☐	☐
11	It frequently occurs that there are problems (malfunctions, defects, breakdowns) with the equipment, the machines, the instruments or the software.	☐	☐
12	There is no regular work consultation, or there are work consultations but they generally do not allow discussion of work problems.	☐	☐
13	It is not, or hardly, possible for employees to determine their own work rate.	☐	☐
14	Within certain broadly defined rules, it is not, or hardly, possible for employees to determine their own working method.	☐	☐

		Yes	No
15	There is insufficient opportunity for employees to help one another, should that be required.	☐	☐
16	The employees receive insufficient information about the results of their work.	☐	☐
17	During working hours, there is insufficient time for a brief chat with colleagues.	☐	☐
18	Frequently, it is not possible to contact the supervisor directly in the event of a problem.	☐	☐
19	Generally, the employees can not directly contact a colleague or supervisor from another department in order to discuss problems.	☐	☐

Total score 'yes' answers: ☐

B. CHECKLIST WORKING CONDITIONS

The Checklist Working Conditions contains 16 questions which can be answered by every department or position. In every case, the answer is either 'yes' or 'no'. The accompanying scores are added up for each position or department.

The higher the total score, the greater the number of problems in the area of working conditions. Every question which results in a '1' indicates an area in which improvements are urgently required.

1	Does the employee spend more than four hours working in a seated position?	yes = 0	no = 1
	If yes, is a good chair provided? If no, is a standing support available?	yes = 0	no = 1
2	Can the employee regularly leave his workplace?	yes = 0	no = 1
3	Does the employee's job require him to work with a continuously bent or twisted posture?	yes = 1	no = 0
4	Must the employee frequently pick up heavy objects or exert a great deal of force?	yes = 1	no = 0
5	Is there sufficient light to perform the work well?	yes = 0	no = 1
6	Are there instances of disturbing reflection or dazzling during the performance of work?	yes = 1	no = 0
7	Are there instances of high or disturbing noise levels in the workplace?	yes = 1	no = 0
8	Is the temperature at the workplace too high or too low?	yes = 1	no = 0

9	Is there an annoying draught in the workplace?	yes = 1	no = 0
10	Are the information points (instruments, lights, sound signals, etc.) easily signalled and understood?	yes = 0	no = 1
11	Are the means of control (buttons, handles, etc.) easily accessible and logically placed?	yes = 0	no = 1
12	Are there dangerous situations in the workplace?	yes = 1	no = 0
13	Are disturbing vibrations experienced in the hand, arm or body during work?	yes = 1	no = 0
14	Are there health risks following exposure to chemical substances?	yes = 1	no = 0
15	Are there risks of infection?	yes = 1	no = 0
16	Are there risks of radiation (for example, radioactive materials, processes)?	yes = 1	no = 0

Total score: ☐

C. CHECKLIST TERMS OF EMPLOYMENT

The Checklist Terms of Employment contains 13 questions which can best be answered by each individual department or position. The checklist can also be used to acquire an image of the terms of employment for the company as a whole. The answers in the right-hand column are added up. The more crosses there are in the right-hand column, the more criticism is directed at the social policy within the company and the bigger the chance that the terms of employment will result in stress. The company should give individual attention to every cross in the right-hand column.

1	Are there sufficient career opportunities?	yes = ☐	no = ☐
2	Are there sufficient education and training opportunities?	yes = ☐	no = ☐
3	Are the jobs in the company under threat, as a result of reorganizations, for example?	yes = ☐	no = ☐
4	Is the remuneration (in money or otherwise) good, compared to similar positions elsewhere?	yes = ☐	no = ☐
5	Can employees determine when their days off are to be taken?	yes = ☐	no = ☐
6	Are the working and resting periods (starting times, finishing times, breaks) well planned?	yes = ☐	no = ☐
7	Are temporary contracts frequently used?	yes = ☐	no = ☐
8	Are temporary workers frequently used?	yes = ☐	no = ☐

9 Are vacancies quickly filled? yes = ☐ no = ☐

10 Can people be replaced during illness? yes = ☐ no = ☐

11 Are there problems with overtime (too much, announced too late, insufficient compensation in time or money, etc.)? yes = ☐ no = ☐

12 Are standard wages or piece rates applied? yes = ☐ no = ☐

13 Are the canteen facilities good? yes = ☐ no = ☐

Total score right-hand column: ☐

D. CHECKLIST SOCIAL RELATIONS AT WORK

The Checklist Social Relations at Work contains 10 questions which can best be answered by each individual department (or position). The checklist can also be used to acquire an image of the company as a whole. A total score for the checklist can be calculated by adding the 'no' answers to the questions 1, 2, 3, 4, 5, 7, and 10, and adding these to the 'yes' answers to the questions 6, 8 and 9. The higher the total score, the greater the number of problems in the area of cooperation, participation problems and within working atmosphere.

Individual attention should be given to every 'no' answer to the questions 1, 2, 3, 4, 5, 7, and 10, and every 'yes' answer to the questions 6, 8 and 9.

		Yes	No
1	Does the daily management give enough consideration to the opinion of the employees?	☐	☐
2	Does the daily management provide sufficient support in the work?	☐	☐
3	Are the employees sufficiently informed of the developments within the company?	☐	☐
4	Is there generally a good atmosphere at the workplace?	☐	☐
5	If necessary, can employees request help from one or more colleagues?	☐	☐
6	Are colleagues monitored too closely in their work?	☐	☐
7	Is there a work consultation system which positions well?	☐	☐
8	Are there instances of discrimination (according to gender, race, etc.)?	☐	☐

		Yes	No
9	Are there instances of sexual harassment?	☐	☐
10	Is there sufficient appreciation for the work that is performed?	☐	☐

Total score: ☐

Source: **Kompier, M.A.J. & Marcelissen**, *F.H.G. Handbook Work Stress* (in Dutch), NIA, Amsterdam (1990).

APPENDIX 2 *Questionnaire Stress at the Work Site*

Instructions:

Please answer each question by checking off the one answer which best fits your job situation. Sometimes neither answer fits exactly. Please choose the answer which comes closest.

1. Are you male or female? ☐ male ☐ female

2. What is your age?

3. How long have you been working for this company? ☐ years

4. What is the highest level of education that you have completed?
   - no formal schooling or primary school ☐
   - completed secondary or high school ☐
   - college or university ☐

5. What type of shift do you work?
   - day shift only ☐
   - two shift ☐
   - three shift ☐
   - four/five shift ☐
   - other ☐

6. What is your job title?
   Be specific:..

7. What business is your company in (i.e. shipbuilding, insurance, etc.)?
   Be specific: ....

Job Demands

		Yes	No
8	My job requires working very fast.	☐	☐
9	My job requires working very hard.	☐	☐
10	I am not asked to do an excessive amount of work.	☐	☐
11	I have enough time to get the job done.	☐	☐
12	I am free from conflicting demands that others make.	☐	☐
13	My job requires long periods of intense concentration.	☐	☐
14	My tasks are often interrupted before they can be completed, requiring attention at a later time.	☐	☐
15	My job is very hectic.	☐	☐
16	Waiting on work from other people or departments often slows me down in my job.	☐	☐

Decision Authority

17	My job allows me to make a lot of decisions on my own.	☐	☐
18	On my job, I have very little freedom to decide how I do my work.	☐	☐
19	I have a lot of say about what happens on my job.	☐	☐

		Yes	No
20	I can determine the order in which my work is to be done.	☐	☐
21	I can determine when a task is to be done.	☐	☐
22	I can easily leave the workplace for a brief period.	☐	☐
23	I can interrupt my work if I so require.	☐	☐
24	I can determine my own work rate.	☐	☐

Skill Discretion

25	My job requires that I learn new things.	☐	☐
26	My job involves a lot of repetitive work.	☐	☐
27	My job requires me to be creative.	☐	☐
28	My job requires a high level of skill.	☐	☐
29	I get to do a variety of different things in my job.	☐	☐
30	I have an opportunity to develop my own special abilities.	☐	☐

Terms of Employment

31	I can determine the moment when I start and stop work.	☐	☐
32	I can determine when I need a break.	☐	☐

		Yes	No
33	I am familiar with my work schedule more than a month in advance.	☐	☐
34	I can determine when I wish to take my days off.	☐	☐
35	My job security is good.	☐	☐
36	My prospects for career development and promotions are good.	☐	☐
37	In five years, my skills will still be valuable.	☐	☐

Supervisor and Co-worker support

		Yes	No
38	The atmosphere at the workplace is good.	☐	☐
39	People at work frequently irritate me.	☐	☐
40	If I so require, I can call in the assistance of one or more colleagues.	☐	☐
41	The daily management under which I work is good.	☐	☐
42	My opinion is sufficiently taken into consideration by the daily management.	☐	☐
43	The daily management has an accurate impression of how I work.	☐	☐
44	The daily management gives me enough support in my work.	☐	☐
45	I am sufficiently informed of the developments within the company.	☐	☐

Scoring and interpretation:

A total score is calculated for each of the modules. If required, these can be divided according to department or position. These groups must include more than 15 respondents, otherwise the averages will become too unreliable and confidentiality can come under threat.

In this manner, it is possible to compare various departments or positions with one another and with the company average.

It is also possible to compare:

- men and women (question 1);
- age groups, e.g. younger and older workers (question 2);
- employees with more or less years of experience in the company (question 3);
- employees with different levels of education/training (question 4);
- employees who work different schedules (question 5);

This is how the total scores are calculated:

Total score Job Demands:

- Questions: 8, 9, 13, 14, 15, 16: yes = 1, no = 0
- Questions: 10, 11, 12: no = 1, yes = 0
- Total score: count all the 'ones' (minimum: 0, maximum: 9).

The higher the total score, the higher the risk of stress.

Total score Decision Authority:

- Questions: 17, 19, 20, 21, 22, 23, 24: yes = 1, no = 0
- Question: 18 yes = 0, no = 1
- Total score: count all the 'ones' (minimum: 0, maximum: 8).

The lower the total score, the higher the risk of stress.

Total score Skill Discretion:

- Questions: 25, 27, 28, 29, 30: yes = 1, no = 0
- Question: 26: no = 1, yes = 0
- Total score: count all the 'ones' (minimum: 0, maximum: 6).

The lower the total score, the higher the risk of stress.

Total score Terms of Employment:

- Questions: 31, 32, 33, 34, 35, 36, 37 (all): yes = 1, no = 0
- Total score: count all the 'ones' (minimum: 0, maximum: 7).

The lower the total score, the higher the risk of stress.

Total score Supervisor and Co-worker support:

- Questions: 38, 40, 41, 42, 43, 44, 45: yes = 1, no = 0
- Question: 39: no = 1, yes = 0
- Total score: count all the 'ones' (minimum: 0, maximum: 8).

The lower the total score, the higher the risk of stress.

Source:

– **R. Karasek**: *Job Content Questionnaire and Users Guide* (1985).

– **P.G.W. Smulders, C.R. de Winter & R.W.M. Gründemann**: T*he Dutch Work and Health Questionnaire (1992)*, TNO Institute for Preventive Health, Leiden (1992).

– **S. Dhondt & I.L.D. Houtman**: *NOVA-WEBA (in Dutch)*, TNO Institute for Preventive Health, Leiden (1992).

– **I.L.D. Houtman, A. Bloemhoff, S., Dhondt, & C. Terwee**: *WEBA and NOVA-WEBA related to health and well-being of employees (in Dutch)*. Den Haag (1994)

The scales of Job Demands, Decision Authority (partly), Skill Discretion, and Terms of Employment (partly), are from the Job Content Questionnaire (Karasek 1985). There is no cost for use. However, permission for use of these scales in large studies (studies with over 500 subjects, or over 150 subjects in a single occupational category) requires that a copy of these data and the demographic data (questions 1-5) be provided to the JCQ Center. Large studies and other interested users are encouraged to contact the JCQ Center for additional information or assistance: JCQ Center, c/o Professor Robert Karasek, Department of Work Environment, University of Massachusetts Lowell, Lowell MA, USA 01854.

APPENDIX 3 *Questionnaire Health Complaints*

Instructions: Please answer each question.

		Yes	No
1	Do you occasionally feel pressure in your stomach or is it ever swollen?	☐	☐
2	Are you quickly short of breath?	☐	☐
3	Do you occasionally feel pain in the chest or heart region?	☐	☐
4	Do you occasionally suffer pain in bones and muscles?	☐	☐
5	Do you frequently feel tired?	☐	☐
6	Do you occasionally suffer a headache?	☐	☐
7	Do you occasionally suffer back complaints?	☐	☐
8	Do you occasionally suffer an upset stomach?	☐	☐
9	Do you ever suffer from a numbed feeling or a tingling sensation in your limbs?	☐	☐
10	Do you tire more quickly than you would expect?	☐	☐
11	Do you occasionally feel dizzy?	☐	☐
12	Do you occasionally feel listless?	☐	☐
13	Do you generally wake up still feeling tired?	☐	☐

Scoring:

The complaints (every yes score) are added up. The minimum score is 0 and the maximum score is 13.

The average complaints level of a company, department or position can easily be calculated. The average can then be compared with that of other positions or departments in the company and/or with external reference groups.

If the questions 1 – 7 from Appendix 2 are combined with the Questionnaire Health Complaints it is also possible to compare men and women, older and younger employees etc.

Source: **J.M. Dirken**: *Dutch Questionnaire VOEG* (in Dutch), TNO-Institute of Preventive Health Care/Wolters Noordhoff, Groningen (1969)

European Foundation for the Improvement of Living and Working Conditions

Stress at work: causes, effects and prevention (guide for small and medium size enterprises)

Luxembourg: Office for Official Publications of the European Communities

1994 – 74 pp. – 14,8 x 21 cm

ISBN 92-826-8594-2

Price (excluding VAT) in Luxembourg: ECU 8.50